COUNTRIES IN OUR WORLD

BRAZIL

IN OUR WORLD

Edward Parker

A⁺

Smart Apple Media

Published by Smart Apple Media
P.O. Box 3263, Mankato, Minnesota 56002

Printed in the United States of America at Corporate
Graphics, in North Mankato, Minnesota.

Published by arrangement with the Watts Publishing
Group Ltd., London.

Library of Congress Cataloging-in-Publication Data

Parker, Edward, 1961-
  Brazil / by Edward Parker.
      p. cm. -- (Countries in our world)
  Summary: "Describes the economy, government, and
culture of Brazil today and discusses Brazil's influence
of and relations with the rest of the world"--Provided
by publisher.
  Includes index.
  ISBN 978-1-59920-441-3 (library binding)
  1. Brazil--Juvenile literature. I. Title.
  F2508.5.P376 2010
  981--dc22

                                    2009031772

Produced by: White-Thomson Publishing Ltd.

Series consultant: Rob Bowden
Editor: Sonya Newland
Designer: Alix Wood
Picture researcher: Amy Sparks

Picture Credits
Corbis: Cover (Gavin Hellier/Robert Harding World
Imagery), 7 (Ben Radford), 9 (Sergio Pitamitz), 14
(Marc Lecureuil), 22 (Paulo Fridman), 24 (Paulo
Fridman), 27 (Robert Maass), 28 (Carlos Cazalis);
Dreamstime: 8 (Tony1), 18 (Mortenelm); iStock: 4,
10, 20; **Edward Parker:** 13, 29; **Photoshot:** 15 (WpN),
25 (WpN); **Shutterstock:** 1 (Celso Pupo), 16 (Pres
Panatoyov), 17 (David Davis), 19 (Rafael Martin-
Gaitero), 21 (Vinicius Tupinamba), 23 (Celso Pupo), 26
(Franck Camhi); **White-Thomson Publishing:** 6, 11, 12.

1207
32010

9 8 7 6 5 4 3 2 1

Contents

Brazil is the fifth largest country in the world. It is slightly smaller than the United States, and has borders with all South American countries except Ecuador and Chile. The largest river in the world, the Amazon, runs through Brazil, and it also has the largest area of unbroken rain forest on the planet.

▼ The statue of Christ the Redeemer towers above Rio de Janeiro, the second largest city in Brazil. The statue has been named one of the New Seven Wonders of the World.

◀ Brazil has international land borders with 10 of the other 12 South American countries— Uruguay, Argentina, Paraguay, Bolivia, Peru, Colombia, Venezuela, Guyana, Suriname, and French Guiana.

A Global Influence for 500 Years

Brazil has had global connections ever since the Portuguese explorer Pedro Cabral arrived there in 1500. The Portuguese cut down Brazil's rare trees to extract a dye from the wood, and dug for minerals such as gold and diamonds. Soon, plantations were established to grow crops, such as sugar and coffee, and slaves were brought from West Africa to provide labor. The plantations made the Portuguese fabulously wealthy and influenced the development of the European economy.

The Rubber Boom

Brazil gained independence in 1822. The Brazilian people began to enjoy their country's wealth for themselves, particularly at the end of the nineteenth century during the "rubber boom." The demand for rubber for vehicle tires was so great that the Amazonian city of Manaus briefly became richer than New York. However, soon after this, the Brazilian economy began to decline. Later, the coffee boom encouraged people from countries such as Italy and Japan to move to Brazil to work.

▲ *Brazil has nearly one-quarter of all the freshwater on Earth flowing through it, which gives it great potential for hydroelectricity.*

The BRIC Countries

In the 1950s, Brazil began a massive development program. The Brazilian government borrowed money from wealthy countries to build factories, roads, ports, and power stations. Today, it is one of the four most important developing nations in the world; these countries are known together as BRIC, which stands for Brazil, Russia, India, and China. They have a major influence on the world because between them, these countries have huge natural resources and more than a third of the world's workforce. As the BRIC countries develop, they are changing the global economy.

Natural Resources

Brazil has a huge wealth of natural resources, including some of the world's largest deposits of iron ore, bauxite (used to make aluminum), diamonds, and gold. Production of many of these resources, especially gold, declined in the 1990s, as restrictions on mining in the Amazon were introduced. Recently, though, investment in mining has increased again. Brazil is also the world's largest producer of sugar, oranges, and beef. However, the country's development has led to the destruction of large areas of rain forest, contributing to global climate change, which is now affecting the whole planet.

BASIC DATA

Official name: **Federal Republic of Brazil**

Capital: **Brasilia**

Size: **3,286,488 sq miles (8,511,965 sq km)**

Population: **198,739,269 (2009 est.)**

Currency: **Real**

FAMOUS BRAZILIAN

Pelé
(b. 1940)

Pelé is one of the most famous living Brazilians. He starred in the 1970 and 1974 soccer World Cup finals, where his brilliance made him a household name around the world. Since retiring from soccer, he has worked to raise awareness of and find solutions to poverty in Brazil.

Brazil Around the World

Brazilian culture has spread around the world, and Brazilian communities can be found in major cities from London to New York. Brazilian art, music, literature, and architecture are now famous throughout the world. Brazil is famous for introducing the rest of the world to the samba dance, bossa nova music, and what many people consider to be the most stylish way of playing soccer.

◀ *Brazilian soccer star Kaká is tackled by England player David Beckham. Kaká was named FIFA World Player of the Year in 2007.*

Brazil is a very large country—so large that it covers nearly half of the entire South American continent, and dominates the economy of the region. The Amazon River runs through the rain forest in the north of the country, and Brazil also has 4,655 miles (7,491 km) of Atlantic coastline.

The Amazon Area

Brazil is divided into five main regions, each of which has its own distinctive landscape and climate. The largest is the Amazon region. It is an enormous area—more than 1.5 million sq miles (3.8 million sq km)—mostly covered in dense tropical rain forest and dominated by water, with thousands of lakes and rivers.

THE HOME OF...

The Amazon River

Every hour, 204,205 gallons (773,000 L) of water from the Amazon River pour into the Atlantic Ocean. At 2.3 million sq miles (6 million sq km), the Amazon also has the largest drainage basin on the planet. With a length of about 4,000 miles (6,437 km), the Amazon is the second longest river in the world, after the Nile River in Africa.

◀ *The Amazon runs through Brazil's rain forest and is the largest river in the world by volume.*

West Central

The West Central is the second largest region in Brazil. Its main feature is a high tableland, or plateau, called the Planalto, which has an average altitude of 3,281 ft (1,000 m) above sea level. The Planalto is largely covered by the Cerrado—a vast area of scrubland. The region also has major deposits of important metals such as gold and nickel.

PLACE IN THE WORLD

Total area: **3,286,488 sq miles (8,511,965 sq km)**

Percentage of world land area: **5.7%**

World ranking: **5th**

Northeast

The Northeast region is located south of the Amazon River and includes a large area of semidesert known as Sertão. This area gets very little rain, so farming is difficult. The coast of the Northeast region is famous for its hot weather, beautiful beaches, and dunes, which make it a major tourist attraction. The coastal strip of the Northeast is ideal for sugar plantations and other tropical crops.

▼ *Tourists enjoy buggy riding in the sand dunes of Genipabu in northeastern Brazil.*

Southeast

The Southeast region covers around 10 percent of Brazil. It is an area of rolling hills with an average altitude of 2,297 ft (700 m) above sea level. This area receives high rainfall, and the land is good for large-scale farming. The Southeast region has metal and mineral deposits, as well as Brazil's most important oil fields. Industry and services are also important to the economy here. The Southeast borders the Atlantic Ocean, and several of Brazil's main cities are located along the coast, including Rio de Janeiro and São Paulo.

South

The South region has gently rolling hills in some areas, which give way to rugged mountains and forested valleys. Some parts of the South are very similar to the Alpine areas of Germany and Italy. The European-style landscape has attracted Italian and German immigrants to cultivate vineyards and set up Brazil's wine industry here. The landscape is well suited to other types of European- and American-style agriculture, including dairy farming to produce milk for the food-processing industry.

▼ *Rio de Janeiro, with its famous natural landmark Sugar Loaf Mountain, is situated on the southeast coast of Brazil.*

Brazil's Climate

Brazil's climate is varied. The Amazon region has a very even climate. It is hot and wet all year round, with daytime temperatures averaging 79°F (26°C) and with an annual rainfall of 59 to 79 in (1,500 to 2,000 mm). Most of the Northeast coast has a warm, tropical climate, with a slightly cooler wet season between May and August, and a hot, dry season between September and April. The Brazilian highlands and plateaus of the Southeast and West Central have distinct seasons, with cool, wet winters, and hot, dry summers. The very south of the country experiences four seasons similar to those in the northern United States.

▲ *Caiman alligators in the Pantanal. This is the largest wetland area in the world—during the rainy season, most of it is underwater.*

THE HOME OF...

The Pantanal

The Pantanal is a vast wetland, which becomes one huge lake almost the size of Texas during the wet season. The main farming activity in the region is cattle ranching, and the area is important for waterfowl, such as scarlet ibis and cormorant. There are also large numbers of caimans, capybara (a giant rodent), marsh deer, jaguars, and giant anteaters.

Environmental Issues

As Brazil's economy develops and its population grows, the country is facing major environmental problems. More factories are causing increased air and water pollution. As more people come to live in Brazil's cities, increased traffic and waste is also causing more pollution. At the same time, parts of the Amazon Rain Forest, Cerrado, and Atlantic forest have been destroyed. This has led to the extinction of some plants and animals, and is now changing the climate of Brazil.

▼ *Large parts of the Amazon Rain Forest have been cleared to make way for plantations. Farming is a vital part of Brazil's economy, but the forest clearance is contributing to global warming.*

FAMOUS BRAZILIAN

Chico Mendes (1944–88)

A rubber-tapper named Chico Mendes became internationally famous when he tried to stop cattle ranchers from cutting down the rain forest in a remote part of the Amazon. He was shot dead by ranchers on December 22, 1988. His death caused an outcry across the world.

Lungs of the World

The Amazon Rain Forest covers more than 2.3 million sq miles (6 million sq km). It is sometimes called "the lungs of the world" because it helps keep the global climate stable. Plants in the Amazon Rain Forest absorb huge amounts of energy from the sun and carbon dioxide (a greenhouse gas) from the air, and release oxygen. When the rain forest is cut down and burned, carbon dioxide is released into the atmosphere, and scientists believe this is playing a part in global climate change. In addition to this, fewer trees means less oxygen is released into the air.

Preventing Pollution

The Brazilian government has responded to the environmental problems by forcing new factories to be designed to produce less pollution. The government has also set up a network of national parks and reserves, covering 3.9 percent of the country, to try to protect rare wildlife. Brazil now produces much of its energy from renewable sources, especially hydroelectric power and biofuels for cars.

> ▶ *This dam, built at the headwaters of the Tocantins River, is one of many new power plants built to produce electricity on tributaries of the Amazon River.*

GOING GLOBAL

Parts of the rain forest and much of the Cerrado are being destroyed to make way for soybean plantations. There is a huge demand for soybeans to feed people in China, as well as dairy cattle in Europe. The needs of other countries are therefore responsible for some of Brazil's environmental problems.

The first Brazilians were the Indians who lived in Amazonia and along the coast. No one knows how many Indians lived in Brazil before the Portuguese arrived in 1500, but it was believed to be millions. Today, there are around half a million Indians in Brazil, belonging to over 200 different tribes.

Slavery in Brazil

After the Portuguese found their way to Brazil in 1500, thousands of Portuguese people moved to the new colony, and many of them married Brazilian Indians. The Portuguese transported millions of slaves from Africa to work on the plantations of sugar and other crops. This had a big effect on the structure of the global population. Africa lost millions of people, and black Africans became a major part of the Brazilian population.

▼ *The Kayopo tribe of Amazonian Indians have fought against deforestation so they can preserve their way of life.*

▲ *The multicultural population can be seen in many parts of Brazil, with descendants of black Africans, European immigrants, and mixed-race people.*

FAMOUS BRAZILIANS

Zumbi
(1655–95)

Zumbi was born into a community of escaped slaves, but was captured by the Portuguese when he was a child. He later escaped and led the fight against slavery in northeast Brazil until he was killed in 1695. Many black Brazilians still honor him as a great warrior and hero.

A Varied Population

Brazil is now the fifth most populated country in the world. There are Amazonian Indians living deep in the rain forest, descendants of the first people of South America. There are also the descendants of African slaves and European people. The mixed-race people from a combination of Indians, Europeans, and black Africans are known as *pardos*. Over the last 100 years, immigrants from many different countries have also moved to Brazil, including people from China, Japan, and Lebanon.

A Young Population

Brazil's population has grown rapidly over the last 50 years, and it now accounts for nearly half of the entire population of South America. Although the rate of growth has slowed in the past 10 years, Brazil's population is still growing by nearly two million people every year. The Brazilian population is very young compared to countries such as the United States, Japan, or Germany—more than a quarter of Brazilians are under 14 years old. This may cause problems because schools must be built to educate them, and jobs must be found as they grow older.

GOING GLOBAL

Brazilian culture is becoming a growing influence in other countries. Samba clubs are numerous, as are *churrascarias*, a type of barbecue restaurant popular in Brazil. New York City even holds an annual New York Brazilian Day Festival in September.

▼ *A Brazilian carnival is celebrated on the streets of Islington, North London. The English capital has a large Brazilian population.*

Population Density

In 2000, the population density of Brazil was 57 people per sq mile (22 people per sq km). However, there are huge differences in population density around the country. For example, 90 percent of Brazilians live within 62 miles (100 km) of the Atlantic coast. São Paulo has a population density of over 9,495 people per sq mile (3,650 people per sq km), whereas in the Amazon region it can be as low as 5 people per sq mile (2 people per sq km).

Moving to the Cities

Fifty years ago, more than two-thirds of people in Brazil lived in the countryside. Today, more than 80 percent live in towns or cities, having moved in search of work and better opportunities. There is a big divide between rich and poor in Brazil, and most of the big cities have slums known as *favelas*, where millions of people live in very poor conditions. Thousands of Brazilians have also left the country in the last 50 years, providing young workers in countries with aging populations such as the United States and the United Kingdom.

▶ *People come to the cities to find work, but often cannot afford housing there, so instead they settle in slums called* favelas *that spring up on the outskirts of the cities.*

PLACE IN THE WORLD

Population: **198,739,269 (2009 est.)**

Percentage of world total: **2.9%**

World ranking: **5th**

Brazil's rich culture today has been influenced by Amazonian Indians, European colonists, and African slaves. In addition, waves of other immigrants from countries such as Germany, Italy, Lebanon, and Japan have influenced Brazilian culture.

Music and Dance

Brazil is famous around the world for its music and dance, especially the samba, which was influenced by the music of the African slaves. The samba has become extremely popular all over the world, and samba-dancing lessons are enjoyed in many different countries.

THE HOME OF...

Carnival

The Rio Carnival—a huge, colorful dance competition held in Rio de Janeiro—has become famous throughout the world. Dozens of samba schools compete against each other for a week in a specially constructed "sambadrome." The Carnival is well-known for its brightly dressed dancers and lively music.

▲ *During the world-famous Rio Carnival, people pack into specially built venues to watch the dancers in brightly colored costumes.*

A Passion for Sports

Brazilians are great sports fans. The Brazilian national soccer team has won the World Cup five times—more than any other country—and introduced a unique style to the sport. Interest in Brazilian soccer skills has meant that many of the great European soccer clubs, such as Real Madrid in Spain and Manchester United in England, have Brazilians on their teams. Brazilians have also been prominent in Formula 1 car racing, with drivers such as Ayrton Senna, Nelson Piquet, and Felipe Massa.

IT STARTED HERE

The Capoeira

Capoeira is an art form that combines martial art and dance. It was developed by African slaves on the sugar plantations. They were forbidden to fight one another, so they invented a type of ritual combat instead.

▼ *In the dance form capoeira, performers take turns singing, playing musical instruments, or "fighting" in the middle of a circle.*

Family Life

Brazilian family life has changed over the last half a century. Fifty years ago, the majority of Brazilian people lived in the countryside, often with—or close to—several generations of their family. Today, the majority of Brazilians live in cities. Millions have moved there in search of work, often leaving their families behind in rural areas. Women make up an increasing number of workers, and there are also more single-parent families than ever before.

THE HOME OF...

Brazil Nuts

All Brazil nuts are still harvested from wild trees that are among the largest that grow in the Amazon Rain Forest. None of the nuts that are transported from Brazil and other South American countries are grown on plantations. Each Brazil nut we eat has been cracked by hand.

Changing Diet

Food is an important part of the Brazilian culture, but feeding more than 198 million people is a major challenge. Beans, rice, coffee, and manioc (a plant with an edible root) are the staple foods for millions of Brazilians. There are many regional variations, with African-style food popular in the Northeast region and European-style cuisine, such as cheese and wine, in the south. Many Brazilian foods are popular around the world, including Brazil nuts and açai juice. However, fast foods, such as burgers and processed foods, are also becoming increasingly popular.

◀ *Fruit juice made from açai berries, which are grown in the Amazon region of Brazil, has become popular all over the world because people believe it has energy-boosting properties.*

Education

Education is free for all children up until the age of 14. However, many children do not complete their education as they may have to work or help their parents look after younger children. It is also free to attend college, but the majority of university students still come from private schools.

Freedom to Choose Religion

Brazil has the second largest number of Christians in the world after the United States. The largest religious group is Roman Catholic, although Protestants are a fast-growing group, representing around one-fifth of the population. The Brazilian constitution states that people have the right to follow a religion of their choice. African Brazilians follow several religions, including Candomblé.

IT'S A FACT!

The Candomblé religion is the best known of the African religions in Brazil, where it has more than a million followers. They believe that everyone has a god (Orixa), which guides and protects them, and followers also worship several other traditional African gods. Candomblé rituals involve dancing and drumming.

▼ *Followers of the Afro-Brazilian religion Candomblé gather by the sea to make offerings to the sea goddess Iemanjá.*

The Brazilian economy has grown rapidly over the last 10 years. Although the rate of growth slowed because of the global economic crisis in 2008, Brazil is still one of the most important trading countries in the world. It is likely to become even more significant in the near future because of its large reserves of natural resources.

Agriculture

Fifty years ago, around half of Brazil's workforce worked in agriculture, but today only around 20 percent are employed in the farming industry. Farming has changed greatly in Brazil. Huge, mechanized "mega farms" have been established in the Southeast and West Central regions of Brazil, and these produce millions of tons of food for people and animals. However, in some parts of Brazil, farms are still small and family-run. Soybeans are the fastest-growing crop because China has an increasing demand to help feed its 1.3 billion people, and a growing economy to pay for it.

▲ *A man tosses freshly harvested coffee beans on a modern coffee plantation.*

GLOBAL LEADER

Farming

Brazil is one of the world's most important farming countries, producing cheap food for the world. It is the leading producer of sugar, coffee, oranges, and beef.

Mining

Brazil is one of the six most important mining countries in the world, with large deposits of bauxite (for aluminum), copper, asbestos, tin, and diamonds. This means that it has an influence on the world economy, as it can choose which countries it wants to trade with in the future. Mineral exports between China and Brazil rose by 525 percent between 1999 and 2003. President Hu of China and President Luiz Inacio Lula da Silva of Brazil met in 2006 and pledged to promote their trade partnership further.

Services

Services are parts of a country's economy that earn money without producing any product, such as tourism and banking. Today, this part of the Brazilian economy employs around two-thirds of the entire workforce.

IT STARTED HERE

Powered Flight

Before what is generally considered to be the first powered air flight by the Wright Brothers in 1903, a Brazilian named Alberto Santos Dumont already had his own personal flying machine—an airship, or blimp. He lived in France and was famous for flying to visit friends. He also liked to dine at Maxim's restaurant in Paris, which he would regularly fly to, tying his small airship to a lamppost outside while he enjoyed his meal.

▼ *Copacabana beach in Rio de Janeiro is a major tourist attraction because of its white sands and lively beach life. All these visitors help boost Brazil's economy.*

Manufacturing

Brazil is a major manufacturing nation, producing a huge range of goods, including vehicles, steel, textiles, and footwear. Many foreign companies, including the United States company Ford and the German company Volkswagen, run factories in Brazil, providing employment for many Brazilian people. In 2004, 9 of the 20 largest companies in Brazil were owned by foreign companies. Brazil ranks sixth in the world for car production.

Imports and Exports

The rapid growth in Brazil's economy over the last 10 years is largely due to the increase in the goods and services that it exports to other countries. For example, the value of Brazil's exports nearly tripled from 2001 to 2007, from US$58 billion to US$161 billion. At the same time, imports grew by 46 percent from US$56 billion to US$121 billion. The main goods that Brazil imports are machinery, electrical equipment, and chemical products.

▼ *Workers weld car frames on an assembly line in Sao Caetano do Sul, in a factory owned by the U.S. company General Motors.*

▲ *This woman is making handbags from imitation leather—actually rubber. This is part of a plan to make money from the rain forest without destroying it.*

IT STARTED HERE

Rubber

Without the discovery and production of rubber, the world's motor industry could have had a very different history. The Portuguese first discovered the Omagua Amazonian Indians using the latex from the rubber tree to waterproof items.
By the end of the nineteenth century, rubber had become a multi-million dollar global industry.

Trading Partners

Brazil's largest single trading partner is the United States, which accounted for 16.1 percent of all exports in 2007. However, when all exports to European countries are added together, it is even larger than that of the U.S. Currently, Argentina accounts for 9.2 percent of Brazilian exports, while China accounts for 6.8 percent, and Japan 3.0 percent.

Brazil was a colony of Portugal for more than 300 years, which meant that the country was mainly run for the benefit of Portugal. This ended with Brazilian independence in 1822, but it was still many years before the country became the republic it is today.

From Empire to Republic

After 1822, Brazil was ruled by emperors, but in 1889, there was a military revolt and the emperor, Pedro II, stepped down. Brazil was declared a republic, but the military really controlled the country. Although there was a period of civilian rule, the army took over again in 1964, and it was not until 1985 that Brazil became a true republic.

The Brazilian Government

Today, Brazil is a presidential republic like the United States. This means that the president is both head of the government and head of state. He is elected directly by the people. Brazil has 26 states, and each one elects its own local government. The National Congress has a president, a federal senate with 81 members, and a 513 seat chamber of deputies.

▼ *The National Congress of Brazil, in the capital Brasilia, was designed by world-famous Brazilian architect Oscar Niemeyer.*

▲ *Children greet a mascot at the 1992 Earth Summit (see box below) to address global environmental problems.*

A New Direction

In 2003, President Lula da Silva came to power. Almost immediately he tried to find ways to reduce the huge gap between rich and poor people in Brazil. He changed Brazilian foreign policy, deciding that it was not good for Brazil to rely too much on Europe and the U.S. for overseas trade. Instead, he began making trade agreements with other developing nations, including China, India, and neighboring South American countries.

IT STARTED HERE

The Earth Summit

The first Earth Summit was held in Rio de Janeiro in 1992. This meeting of United Nations countries was intended to work out ways to solve global environmental problems. Representatives from 172 nations attended the summit, and it influenced environmental policies all over the world.

By 2020, Brazil's population may reach 210 million. Compared to countries in Europe and North America, it will still have a young population and a large workforce, which will give it an economic advantage over countries with older populations. However, there is the potential for unrest because of the huge gap between rich and poor people in Brazil.

Boom or Bust?

Many developing nations may face economic problems because they are using up too many of their natural resources. This is unlikely to happen in Brazil because it has such large reserves of so many resources that it will be able to provide its industries with the materials they need. This may lead to an increasing influence on the global economy.

GLOBAL LEADER

Biofuels

After World War II (1939–45), the Brazilian government decided that it wanted to reduce its imports, such as oil. It developed an industry producing alcohol from sugar cane (biofuel) for cars. Today, Brazil is a world leader in biofuel production, and around 20 percent of Brazilian vehicles run on biofuel.

◀ *This man is harvesting sugar cane, which will be used as a biofuel. This fuel is cheap to produce and less polluting than gasoline or diesel.*

Deforestation and Climate Change

Brazil could suffer from environmental disaster if some of the major problems are not addressed. Deforestation in the Amazon is causing changes in weather patterns in Brazil and across the world. A change in temperature or rainfall in the large agricultural areas could be disastrous for crops. Also, some cities are already using more water than is locally available. However, Brazil has huge potential for producing renewable energy, such as hydroelectric power, solar power, and biofuel.

▲ *Limiting deforestation in the rain forests, while still developing its economy, is the most pressing problem Brazil faces in the near future.*

IT'S A FACT!

Brazil is already the tenth largest economy in the world. If it continues to grow at the same rate as it has for the past 10 years, it will probably overtake Spain and Italy by 2020, and possibly even France and the United Kingdom.

Glossary

biofuel a fuel usually made from a plant material, such as wheat for ethanol.

Candomblé a religion practiced in Brazil that has African origins.

Capoeira a type of slow-motion dancing and fighting developed by African slaves in Brazil.

churrascaria a type of barbecue restaurant that originated in Brazil, but is now popular all over the world.

constitution the written laws [agreed general principles] of a formal organization, such as a national government.

drainage basin an area of land that contributes water to a stream or river.

economy the financial system of a country or region, including how much money is made from the production and sale of goods and services.

export to send or transport products, materials, or services abroad for sale or trade.

extinction the dying out of a particular species of plant or animal.

favelas a Brazilian word for slums or shanty towns, which are often found on the outskirts of the big cities.

global warming the gradual rise in temperatures on the surface of the Earth caused by changes in the amount of greenhouse gases in the atmosphere.

greenhouse gas any of several gases that trap warmth in the atmosphere, which can contribute to global warming if too much is generated on Earth.

import to bring in goods or materials from a foreign country for sale.

manioc a root crop like a potato or a yam, which originally grew in the Amazon, but is now grown industrially. Also known as cassava.

pardos a word describing mixed-race Brazilian people with white, black, and Indian ancestry.

Planalto a high plateau in the West Central region of Brazil.

plantation a large area where crops, such as coffee or sugar cane, are grown in orderly rows.

rain forest a forest that receives more than 3.3 ft (1 m) of rainfall spread evenly throughout the year.

republic a political system whose head of state is a president who has been elected by the people.

resources things that are available to use, often to help develop a country's industry and economy. Examples include minerals, workers (labor), or water.

Sertão a large area of semidesert in the Northeast region of Brazil.

Further Information

Books

The Amazon Rain Forest
Nature's Wonders
by Ann Heinrichs
(Marshall Cavendish
Benchmark, 2009)

Brazil
Countries of the World
by Zilah Deckker
(Wash. D.C. National
Geographic Society, 2008)

Brazil
Destination Detectives
by Ali Brownlie Bojang
(Raintree, 2007)

Brazil
Country Explorers
by Elizabeth Weitzman
(Lerner Publications, 2008)

Brazil
Enchantment of the World
by Ann Heinrichs
(Children's Press/Scholastic, 2008)

Brazil
Travel Through
by Joe Fullman
(QEB Publishing, 2007)

Web Sites

**https://www.cia.gov/library/publications/
the-world-factbook/geos/br.html**
A good source of general statistics about Brazil.

http://www.saopaulo.sp.gov.br/
The web site of the São Paulo State government.

http://www.brasilemb.org
The Brazilian embassy in Washington D.C.

http://www.governo.rj.gov.br
Information on Rio de Janeiro.

*Every effort has been made by the publisher to ensure
that these web sites contain no inappropriate or offensive
material. However, because of the nature of the Internet,
it is impossible to guarantee that the contents of these sites
will not be altered. We strongly advise that Internet access
is supervised by a responsible adult.*

Index